50 Deliciously Simple DIY Lip Balm Recipes: Make Your Own Lip Balm From Natural Ingredients Today

Jennifer N. Smith

Copyright © 2020 Jennifer N. Smith

All rights reserved.

ISBN: 9798649454001

Copyright

All rights reserved. No part of this Book may be reproduced or transmitted in any form or by any means, electronic or mechanical, including photocopying, recording or by any information storage and retrieval system, without written permission from the author.

Disclaimer

The recipes and information in this book are provided for educational purposes only. Please always consult a licensed professional before making changes to your lifestyle or diet.

The author and/or publisher shall have neither liability nor responsibility to anyone with respect to any loss or damage caused, or alleged to be caused, directly or indirectly by the information contained in this book. All trademarks and brands within this book are for clarifying purposes only and are owned by the owners themselves, not affiliated with this document.

50 Deliciously Simple DIY Lip Balm Recipes: Make Your Own Lip Balm From Natural Ingredients Today

Table of Contents

Introduction 4

50 Deliciously Simple DIY Lip Balm Recipes 5

1. Basic Homemade Lip Balm 5

2. Coconut Vanilla Lip Balm 7

3. Honey and Lavender Lip Balm 9

4. Lavender Lip Balm 11

5. Natural Shimmering Lip Balm 13

6. Shea Butter Lip Balm 15

7. Peppermint Lip Balm 17

8. Chocolate and Rose Lip Balm 19

9. Mint chocolate Lip Balm 21

10. Chocolate Truffle Lip Balm 23

11. Glittery 4-Ingredient Lip Balm 25

12. Coconut and Beeswax 27

13. Minty Lip Balm 28

14. Raspberry and Lemon 30

15. Pure Essentials Lip Balm 31

16. Rosy Lip Balm 33

17. Hemp and Honey 35

18. Organic Shea Butter Lip Balm 37

19. Kool-Aid Lip Balm 39

20. Limey Lip Balm..40

21. Yummy Grapefruit Lip Balm 42

22. Maple Syrup Lip Balm 44

23. Orangey Vanilla Lip Balm 46

24. Lavender Mint Lippy 48

25. Easy Lip Balm 50

26. Two Ingredient Lip Balm 51

27. Cupcake Lip Balm 53

28. Crystal Light Lip Balm...55

29. Simply Lime Lip Balm 56

30. Raspberry Lip Balm (with Real Raspberries) 58

31. Plumping Lip Balm 60

32. Tangy Lemony Raspberry Balms..62

33. Natural Hemp and Honey Lip Balm 63

34. Wedding Favor Lip Balms...65

35. Sparkly Strawberry Lip Balm 66

36. Simple Pink Lip Balm..67

37. Coconut Rose Lip Balm..68

38. Cool Refreshing Lip Balm 69

39. Simple Three Ingredient Lip Balm 70

40. Bottle Cap Lip Balm..71

41. Mint and Shea Butter Lip Balm 72

42. Swirly Lip Balm 73

43. Simple DIY Lip Balm 75

44. Birthday Cake Lip Balm 76

45. Minty Chocolate Lip Balm with REAL chocolate 78

46. Two-Tone Lip Balm 80

47. Brownie Lip Balm 82

48. Coconut Honey Lip Balm 83

49. Heart Lip Balms 84

50. Blueberry Lip Balm 86

Tips for Lip Balm Creation 88

The Best Lip Balm Ingredients 90

Cautions with homemade lip balms 93

Conclusion 95

Introduction

Do you like lip balms?

Lip balms are great to help with your lips if you have chapped lips. But did you know that they're a key part of maintaining lip health? Dry lips happen even when it's hot outside, and it can be quite frustrating to have to buy one a lot.

They rack up in price, and with many of the traditional lip balms, you end up getting a lot of extraneous chemicals that you may not want in your product. If that's the case, it's time for you to start learning how to make your own.

Homemade lip balms end up solving this issue completely, allowing you to invest in a personal item that you made yourself, and it has the benefit of treating your lips in a more natural means. This book provides ten different recipes that allow you to get the benefits of this, and you'll be able to easily, and without many problems, get to use the lip balms that you want.

So what are you waiting for? It's time for you to try using these homemade lip balms, and by the end of this, you'll have ten different options that you'll surely love.

50 Deliciously Simple DIY Lip Balm Recipes

1. Basic Homemade Lip Balm

First, let's discuss the basic homemade lip balm. This is similar to the Burt's Bee's stuff, but it is a bit different. It's cheaper, and all natural. It's quite easy to make, but you will need a few things. However, if you plan on making a lot of this, it's much cheaper in the long run. How to make it will be discussed below, along with a few helpful tips and tricks.

Ingredients:

- 2 tablespoons beeswax
- 2 tablespoons Shea butter
- 2 tablespoons Coconut oil
- 30 drops at least of Peppermint essential oil
- Tubes for it
- A pipette to fill the tubes
- A double boiler

Directions:

- Take the beeswax, coconut oil, and Shea butter and melt all of these in a double boiler, stirring until it's fully melted.
- Take it off the heat, but keep it over the water to keep it melted.

- Add in the essential oils you want, such as peppermint. Do a few drops, test it, and then add it to your liking. Use it on your arm to ensure the scent is what you want.

- Take the dropper and put it in the tubes. You need to do this quickly since it gets removed before it hardens.

- From here let the tubes sit for a few hours until they're totally hardened and from there, you'll cap them.

If you use more beeswax, you'll be able to get a thicker lip balm that lasts a bit longer, but ideally just throw down an extra teaspoon or so.

You also can re-melt these and add more of an ingredient during the process of melting in order to give you a texture that works for you. You can experiment with these, and if you're worried about whether or not it fits, take a small amount of this, throw it in the fridge, and let it harden.

This basic lip balm is a great option if you're looking to truly master the art of creating a fun lip balm, and it's a good one to begin with if you want to get into this as well.

2. Coconut Vanilla Lip Balm

Coconut oil is a very popular carrier oil for many people to use in their lip balms. That's because it helps to enrich the softness of the skin for a long time. Plus, coconut oil contains Vitamin E, which is essential if you want to have soft and silky lips that look beautiful. You can also help to moisturize your lips with coconut oil too.

Coconut oil is great because it doesn't disrupt the skin layers on the lips, and it does help to provide comfort in there. Compared to the ones with a bunch of chemicals, coconut oil is the winner, and this chapter will discuss how to make coconut oil vanilla lip balms that work wonders.

Ingredients:

- About 2 tablespoons of virgin coconut oil
- A teaspoon of vanilla extract
- 2 tablespoons of cocoa butter or mango butter, whichever you want
- 2 tablespoons of beeswax

Directions:

- If you need to chop or grate the beeswax, do so.
- measure this out so that it's got equal parts of the beeswax and butters into a measuring cup.
- Add in the coconut oil and prepare a double boiler. You should get the bottom of the jar itself into there. Heat it until it melts, and stir it

occasionally. You should make sure the water doesn't boil over or blend into the contents.

- Once it's melted, put the vanilla extract in there. Do make sure that you're careful when handling this, since it's hot.

- The mixture should be hot, so put it into either the lip balm containers or tubes or tubs, whichever you want. Put them in the fridge to set.

- This makes about 15 containers, so you'll have a lot to try out, and many different kinds for yourself!

Vanilla lip balms are great, and with the addition of coconut oil, you'll be able to utilize these to the perfect level. Create the lip balms that you want easily, and by adding coconut oil, you can moisturize the lips in the ways you want to.

3. Honey and Lavender Lip Balm

Lavender is a great addition to your lip balms, because they're quite healing and soothing to the area. Lavender is great for chapped lips, since it helps with easing the occurrence of it. Plus, honey is really good for this, and if you use raw honey, it's all natural and soothing. You can make these homemade lip balms if you want to, and this chapter will tell you how to do so.

Ingredients:

- A teaspoon of some Shea butter
- A teaspoon of some sweet almond oil
- Two tablespoons of coconut oil
- A teaspoon of raw honey
- Two tablespoons of beeswax
- 5 drops of frankincense oil
- 15 drops of lavender oil
- Lip balm tubes if you want to put it in there

Directions:

- Take the lids off the tubes and put them together with a rubber band.

- Take the oils along with the beeswax and put them in a heatproof container, and then into a pot of water. Create a double boiler to melt this.
- Once melted, you take it off the heat.
- From here, you put in the essential oils, along with the honey, mixing this together until it's all incorporated.
- Once finished, you take the mixture and put it into the tubes.
- From there, let the lip balms set. You can speed this up by throwing it into the fridge. From there, you can cap and store the containers, or give them to others as gifts.

These are great lip balms, and usually with this recipe, you have enough to last you about a year. They're also non-toxic, so if you do have kids or pets and they accidentally get into them, or if you're worried about abnormalities, you don't have to worry, since they are nontoxic. Plus, the scent is enough to enjoy as well.

4. Lavender Lip Balm

With this, you can create a great lavender lip balm that works for you. With this as well, you can also substitute various essential oils or scents with one another. For example, in this one we will discuss mint, but you can also use rose, chamomile, vanilla, and even sweet orange. This one also incorporates some can include honey, so if you want to throw that in, just put a couple of tablespoons in there.

It's also very soft, and if you put it in a lip balm tube, it does hold up well. Some people like to use the tubes again, so if you do so, you can sterilize them in water that's boiling for a few minutes before you add in the new flavor.

These take about 20 mins to make, and usually make about 7-9 different lip balm for you to use.

Ingredients:

- About a tablespoon of some coconut oil
- 2 tablespoons of Shea butter
- 7 drops of lavender oil
- 1 tablespoon of beeswax
- 7 drops of peppermint
- Containers and tubes
- You can use other types of essential oils as well if you want to use something a bit different. Of course, this is ultimately up to you.

Directions:

- Take a small pot that's on medium low heat and have some water in there. From there, create a double boiler with a Pyrex glass cup or something that's heatproof.

- Take the beeswax, butter, and the oil and melt all of this together, mixing it from time to time to make sure it's all put together.

- From here, take this off the heat and add in the oils of your choice. Use a whisk or something to stir this in order to distribute it all throughout.

- Take this and carefully put it into the containers. Do this quick though, because it does cool down fast. If you do end up messing it up however, you can always re-heat it, melt it, and then try again to see what will happen.

- Put them on the counter or the fridge, and from there, let them sit there until they're hard. Then, you can use it!

That's all there is to it! For many people, it's a simple, and fun way to truly get the benefits that you want out of this. By taking your time and trying out the lavender flavor, and even mixing it with different types, you'll be able to create the perfect lavender lip balm of your choice, and one that does create a great result as you do use this.

5. Natural Shimmering Lip Balm

One type of lip balm people like to make is a shimmering lip balm. You probably remember as a kid maybe getting those lip balms that shimmer. Well, those also have a ton of chemicals in them, and it's actually something that you probably shouldn't put so near your body. But, you can make your own, with a natural ingredient that changes the way things are. What is it? Well, it's natural mica powder, and we will go over what that is, and how it relates to creating shimmering lip balms.

Now, before you do this, you should make sure that you have the lip balm tubes cleaned out. You can also add color here with some cocoa powder, but if you just want a plain color, you don't have to do that. Usually, the mica gives it a rose color tone.

So What is Mica?

Well, mica is a silicate mineral that actually is very colorful. There are so many options, and it's safe, but also not toxic as well. Mica is a great one to experiment with in some of the different homemade products out there, but with lip balms, it gives a shimmer, and a little bit of color, and in fact, it can actually brighten the face and the lips without the aid of makeup and other chemicals.

There are a lot of nasty chemicals in lip balms that are commercially made, and it also even contains other unsavory ingredients including ambergris which is whale vomit, and cochineal beetles, which are basically beetles that are used to make red dye in makeup. Simply put, you may not know what you're getting, and that's why many flock to these homemade alternatives.

So how do you make this? Well, read on to find out!

Ingredients:

- 1 tablespoon of Shea or cocoa butter, depending on what color you want
- 1/2 teaspoon of mica powder color that you want to use
- 1 tablespoon coconut oil
- 1 tablespoon beeswax pastilles
- 15 drops of peppermint essential oil

Directions:

- Create a double boiler and from there, melt the oil, the butter, and the beeswax that you have over a medium heat.
- When it's finished melting, do stir it, and then turn off your heat.
- Put in the mica powder and essential oils that you've decided to use (again essential oils can be optional here if you are sensitive to them.)
- Use a dropper or a pipette to put the mixture into containers that are empty. You need to do this quickly before it hardens up, so don't be too slow.
- Let these sit on the counter for about an hour until they're completely hardened.
- From here, you can take them out, and then use them as your own traditional lip balm!

The cool thing about mica, is that you can mix and match different colors with this. For example, you can create a beautiful color using red and gold, but lots of times, you can choose for yourself what color you want. It's fun, and gives a little bit of extra pizzazz to this, so if you want to create a more pigmented sort of lip balm, this is definitely the way to go, and it gives a beautiful natural shimmer that you will enjoy.

6. Shea Butter Lip Balm

Shea butter is a great addition to anyone's lips. It's something that you can use on your own, but combined with coconut oil and beeswax, it creates the ultimate lip balm. Once you try this, you'll never want to go back to your old lip balm.

That's because it actually creates a barrier around your lips, which naturally helps to protect it from the elements. If you live in a place with a lot of cold weather, or even dry weather, chances are your lips are probably affected by it. If that's the case, this is essential for you, and you can use it naturally to help with chapped lips and cracks as well.

It's also rich in vitamins E, A, and F, along with other minerals, which is used to naturally help soothe, balance out, and hydrate your lips. It also does help you with creating a healthy look, and it can even help with protection against many factors. Plus, it's natural, and doesn't have chemicals ridden within it, so it's definitely the way to go.

How do you make this? Well, read on to find out. The cool thing about this, is that it literally takes only a few minutes to prepare this, and then, you'll have natural lip protection that you'll love, and one that works for you too.

Ingredients:

- A 30% natural emulsifier
- 70% oil Phases
- 2 teaspoons of organic sweet almond oil
- 2 teaspoons organic castor oil

- 3 tablespoons beeswax pellets
- 2 teaspoons of refined Shea butter, organic
- 1 tablespoon of coconut oil, organic
- 10 drops of organic lavender essential oil if you want that in there
- 10 plastic tubes to put the mixture in

Directions:

- First thing you do is of course, take the beeswax and the oil and combine them together into a container, and heat up a pot. Put the container with the oils on top of it in order to create a double boiler, melting this.
- Once that's finished, take it off, and you can mix in the essential oils if you want that, or just put it directly into the containers. Again, do this fast as said before because that tends to harden quicker than you may expect.
- If you do notice it hardening though, take the container, turn it on to low heat again, and melt it, and from there, transfer it once more into the containers.
- Once that's done, let this sit on the counter in order to harden again, and then there you have it!

As you can see, it's super easy to make these, and you'll be able to create and take care of your lips in a simple manner with these homemade lip balms. Shea butter is so good for the lips, and having it in a small tube will immediately nourish and help take care of the skin in a simple manner, allowing you to have a healthier life, and a much healthier set of lips too in order to protect them from the elements that are out there.

7. Peppermint Lip Balm

Peppermint is a great element to incorporate into your lip balms. That's not just because it helps with soothing, relieving dried lips, and protects against the elements, it's actually great for something else, a benefit that few talk about.

That's plumping up your lips. Having a full set of pouty lips is something people want, and with peppermint oil, you can create that. That's because the peppermint oil in these lip balms gets on the lips and stimulates your circulation. This in turn creates a small "swell" against the lips to make them fuller as well.

Now, there are some organic lip balms that do this, but let's be real, those get expensive, and with just a few ingredients, and a little bit of time, you too can create a beautiful set of full lips using these lip balms. How? Well, read on to find out.

It creates revitalizing feeling in the person, and it's a wonderful addition to any lip balm collection.,

Ingredients:

- 4 tablespoons of some beeswax pellets, white
- 6 tablespoons of almond oil
- 4 tablespoons of coconut oil
- 6-10 drops of peppermint essential oil

Directions:

- Take a saucepan and fill it about halfway with water, and then let it sit down to boil. You'll want to make sure that the pot isn't super deep, because you want the jar in there to sit on the water itself to create a double boiler and not get water into the jar you're going to use.
- With this, you can use either a mason jar, or any type of container that's heatproof, and from there, throw in the beeswax and the oils together into there. Once you've got boiling water, you can set them into the water itself.
- Let the ingredients sit in there to melt, and use a chopstick, or a stirring stick in order to mix it all together.
- Once you have the mixture clear and everything is melted, take it out of the heat, put the oil in, and stir it.
- Take the containers and then slowly and carefully put the mixture into there. You should use an oven glove because the container can be super hot, and you don't' want to scald yourself. You can pour it in evenly.
- Let it sit on the counter and then let it solidify. At this point, you can use it, and then you can keep the rest to the side for when you run out.

If you want to make this tinted, you can take a lip color, put a bit into there, and add it in as the oils melt. Either that, or mica powder if you want to create the shimmer. It's so easy, and you will be able to create different variants. You can also use normal beeswax pellets if you're not into the look of the white ones.

Peppermint is a great addition to virtually anyone's homemade lip balm kit, and this chapter showed you how you can make this.

8. Chocolate and Rose Lip Balm

Have you ever had a lip balm that smells like both chocolate and roses? Well, now you can have it, with this amazing recipe. Rose is so good for the lips, and that's because it can soothe and cool the area, so if you've got lips that are dried or sunburned, this is perfect for it. You can also get rose essential oil to help with treating cracked lips, and even cold sores, since it keeps everything nice and moisturized.

Rose petals in oil can actually create a beautiful scent, and it definitely does create a nice extra touch. You can use this to soothe your lips, and roses in particular are the best with it. If you do use this, you get a beautiful reddish color. You can use dried roses for this for an extra touch. Some like to substitute hibiscus for this, and that creates a pink lip balm. Again, you can experiment with this.

The cocoa butter you use with this actually makes it almost like you're getting chocolate and roses, and this can create a valentine's day feeling right with your lip balm. It's also a great moisturizer as well.

Ingredients:

- 2 tablespoons of coconut oil
- 1 tablespoon dried rosebuds
- 3 drops of rose essential oil, and some vanilla and lavender oil for an extra touch
- 1 tablespoon grated cocoa butter
  1/4 teaspoon vitamin E oil

Directions:

- Take the ingredients, and on very low heat, melt down your coconut oil into a stainless-steel pot or a bowl. You can also use a heatproof glass too.
- You can then take the roses and stir them in. Let them steep for about an hour, and then strain this through a sieve until you've just got the liquid.
- Wipe down the original heating pot, and then put the oil back in, heat it up, and then add in the cocoa butter until it's fully melted.
- From here, remove it from the heat, add in some vitamin E, and some of the essential oils and then stir it completely.
- Put this quickly into the containers, and if it starts to harden, put it back on the heat to melt for a minute, and then let this set for about 3 hours or so, or until it's fully hardened.

And there you have it! Rose is a great addition, and you can use this to give it a chocolatey and rosy goodness that you will enjoy, and one that will create a great feeling on your lips, and can help to soothe them as well.

9. Mint chocolate Lip Balm

If you're a fan of mint and chocolate, this is actually a great one. It's also a good one for Christmas as well, and makes a great gift. This one is a good one to use with tubes, since it can be very firm and doesn't apply well with a tin. You can rub it around for a bit though until it's soft enough.

Cocoa powder doesn't give it a ton of color, since it'll make it tan. You can try to increase the amount in there, but also be careful so that you don't overwhelm the minty smell. As for the mint, it's a really great smell, and mint is so refreshing for the lips that many people will enjoy. It's definitely a good one to have to help soothe the skin there. Ideally, don't lick your lips doing this, since it can cause the skin to dry out quicker and defeats the purpose of this lip balm.

It's very invigorating, and it helps to soothe out the skin, making it perfect for the colder months, or when the air becomes dry.

Ingredients:

- 1 ounce of beeswax
- 2-3 drops of carrotseed oil
- 1/4 teaspoon of honey
- 1/4 cup of coconut oil
- 3 tablespoons of cocoa butter

Directions:

- The first thing you need to do is if you decide to mix in cocoa butter with Shea butter, you can, just make sure to mix the equal parts. The

Shea provides moisture and the cocoa gives it the chocolaty taste to it. Again, the Shea is optional though. You can also do mango too if you like that.

- Take the butter and mix it with the coconut oil and let it sit in a double boiler system until you get the mixture to about 175 degrees and melted. Let it sit there for 20 minutes, and let it stir occasionally, adding in beeswax too.

- Remove from heat, and then add in the essential oils. Some like to use just mint, and others like to add in different ones as well. If you want a deeper brown color, use more cocoa butter to help make it darker. You should from here put it into the containers quickly.

- Let this sit down to harden, and once it's fully hard, use it. You'll immediately smell the delightful minty taste, and you'll also enjoy the chocolate in there as well. Pair it with these other butters and the coconut oil makes it for the ideal lip balm for not just a beautiful scent, but also to help heal the lips whenever you need it.

This is a great and simple lip balm that allows for a lot of modifications, and many different things that you can do with it that you'll enjoy.

10. Chocolate Truffle Lip Balm

Do you like the taste of chocolate truffles? Do you want to have it in your lip balm? Well, now you can. It really only takes about five ingredients to make this, and it's super simple to do. Some of these have been discussed about already, such as cocoa butter, Shea butter, and beeswax, but two of the other ones, such as sweet almond oil and vanilla oil, are a bit different and deserve a mention.

Sweet almond oil is another nourishing oil. You can substitute it though for avocado, grapeseed, or apricot kernel depending on what you want. It's good for the lips and soothes them.

Vanilla gives it the whipped texture and taste, and it's a great one for the lips too, since it not only smells good, but mixes well with the cocoa.

To make this, you just have to follow the directions below and read the recipe regarding this.

When you do pour these in, always make sure they are poured to the point where it overflows, since it can actually shrink and the hole in the middle happens. If you're going to just use these on your own though, you don't have to worry too much about it. It's hard to completely fill it, but try your best.

Ingredients:

- 2 tablespoons of beeswax
- 1 tablespoon of Shea butter
- 20 drops of vanilla oil
- 3 tablespoons cocoa butter

- 2 tablespoons sweet almond oil

Directions:

- To begin, you make a double boiler as mentioned before by taking a bowl, and then putting it into boiling water
- Put in the butters, oil, and the beeswax together into the double boiler, melting it and stirring it until everything is mixed together and melted. From here, add in the cocoa butter and stir it in as well until everything is fully melted.
- From here, you should take it off the heat, and put the vanilla oil into there, mixing it all together until it starts to fully incorporate.
- From here, put it all into the tubes, and then, cool everything down completely. You can then use this to create a great lip balm recipe, and it's one that people will not only enjoy, but it's one that has the taste of truffle right at your disposal.

Truffles are great, and you can take them, along with the taste of chocolate, into a succulent lip balm with this fun recipe.

11. Glittery 4-Ingredient Lip Balm

Do you want to make a simple, yet effective lip balm for you or your teen or tween? Well now you can. Anyone will love these. They are quite simple to make, and you can do it together, or make it for someone. In this, we'll give you a simple procedure for you to try. By the end of this, you'll have a great and really effective means to get the results you want, and it's so simple that practically anyone could do this.

Ingredients:

- Some coconut oil
- Some beeswax
- Essential oils of choice
- Edible glitter or edible luster
- Optional: lip tint to add an extra color to it

Directions:

- To begin use a 3:1 ratio of coconut oil to beeswax, combining this into a small bowl. Microwave this for about 30 seconds and then continue to do this in increments until everything is melted.
- Stir to combine, then let it sit and cool for 5 minutes
- Add in the essential oils and the lip tint of choice to this. make sure everything's thoroughly integrated together in order to make sure that you have the proper combination for everything.
- Add in the glitter along with the luster dust to the mixture, and then mix it together until combined

- Let it settle in the mixture and stir it together until thoroughly incorporated before you divide this into small containers that can be used to hold it
- Either leave it out to cool down or put it in the fridge to let this set before you do decide to use it

This is a safe and effective lip balm mixture that's guaranteed to provide softer lips and a bit of shimmer too. It is natural and safe, and definitely something that you should consider especially if you want to give your teen something simple, yet effective.

12. Coconut and Beeswax

Coconut and beeswax are two other great ingredients that are simple to use. Not only that, they are great for hydrating the lips too. This recipe is simple to follow, and it only requires a few ingredients.

Ingredients:

- A tablespoon of grated beeswax
- A dash of raw honey, preferably organic
- A tablespoon of coconut oil
- 2 vitamin E capsules

Directions:

- Use the double boiler method where you have a dish or container over a pot in order to melt, he beeswax. When it's half melted, add the coconut oil and the honey
- Blend these ingredients together until mixed add two more capsules of vitamin E oil
- Once this has cooled down, transfer this to a tin or a container
- Use it whenever your lips feel dehydrated.

This is a good one because it is mostly unscented or not super strong in terms of scent, but it also provides both coconut along with beeswax to the person, which is a wonderful combination. You can also mix in some other ingredients too. This one is also good for hydration, since a lot of people struggle with properly hydrating their lips.

13. Minty Lip Balm

This simple lip balm combines the succulent and sweet taste of mint chocolate into a beeswax lip balm. It also has a nutty texture to it too due to the use of the sweet almond oil, which differs from the other mint chocolate lip balm which is present here on the list. If you're a fan of peppermint, and like the cool, refreshing taste, this is a good one.

Ingredients:

- 2 teaspoons of white beeswax pellets
- 2 teaspoons of sweet almond oil
- 1 teaspoon cocoa powder
- A couple drops of peppermint oil

Directions:

- Get the double boiler in place again and from there melt the beeswax pellets. You can also do this in the microwave too
- Add in the cocoa powder until fully blended, and then after that, add in the rest of the ingredients together.
- From there, stir to combine, and as it cools down, put it in some storage contains. For faster cooling, you can put it in the fridge.
- From there, use this lip balm in order to hydrate. It has a wonderful taste, and is quite potent, so a little bit goes a long way with this one.

This one is great especially if you're a fan of mint. However, do be careful with this. sometimes if it's too minty, it can be a bit overpowering. It's important to make sure that you do test a little bit of it on your skin. If you need to mix it to dilute it further, don't be afraid to add more almond oil to this, since it is a carrier oil. Otherwise, have fun with it! It's a refreshingly simple lip balm that's definitely worth trying out, and it's perfect for if you're looking for a simple lip balm to bring around with you, and it's got a nice, dark color to it as well.

14. Raspberry and Lemon

You might think this combo is a bit strange, but it works well. Raspberry is sweet, while lemon brings that extra kick to the table that a lot of people love with their lip balms. Luckily, you can get this together, and you don't have to use too many ingredients to get the effect.

Ingredients:

- 2 tablespoons raspberry gelatin mix
- 4 drops of lemon oil, preferably lemon essential oil
- 2 tablespoons virgin coconut oil

Directions:

- To begin, you start by heating up the coconut oil in a microwave-safe bowl for about 20 seconds or so.
- Add in the raspberry mix and from there mix it together until blended.
- From there, microwave it again until the gelatin begins to melt. The oil should have a raspberry look to it.
- Add in the lemon and begin to mix this completely until properly blended.
- Let this cool down and then pour it into the lip balm container. Place it in the fridge till it hardens up.

This combination works pretty well, but if you do find the lemon too sour for your tastes, you can always add in a little bit more raspberry in order to dilute it. But if you like the zesty flavor of lemon, you're also more than welcome to add more to the mixture too for best results.

This is a good one especially if you want something a little bit fruitier for your lips. You certainly will get a fun, really immersive taste from it, and is great if either of these flavors are some of your favorites, that's for sure.

15. Pure Essentials Lip Balm

This is a lip balm that's made with essential oils of choice. The cool thing about this is that you don't need to do much to get the desired effect from this. in fact, it only involves a little bit of ingredients, and it's a bit different from the rest of the options out there.

It's partially because you can add your own variety of flavors to it, and you don't have as many constrains as the other lip balms on the list.

To begin, follow the instructions and get the ingredients below.

Ingredients:

- 1/4 cup of mango or cocoa butter
- A few drops of an essential oil of choice that you like
- A little bit of beeswax or soy wax
- 1 teaspoon beetroot powder

Directions

- Melt the soy wax or the beeswax in your double boiler.
- Add in the mango or coca butter into that and then blend it with the beeswax.

- Put in the essential oils that you like such as peppermint or even grapefruit. You can get creative with this, so long as it isn't toxic to the body.
- If you're looking to add a bit of powder, add the ground beetroot powder and stir it together until it's not lumpy.
- From there, let this calm down and then put it into some containers carefully, making sure that you don't have anything too large in it.

With this one, you can be a bit more creative than with the others, which is of course, one of the major benefits to it. The sky's your limit in terms of the types of things you can do with this, and the fun you can have.

You can mix in more flavors if you feel like it would do well for the lip balm itself. This one does come with a fruitier taste, since it does come with the mango butter. Mango butter offers a more tropical taste, while normal cocoa butter has a bit of a cocoa taste to it, which makes it sweeter. But you can mix in whatever you want, and even mix both of these butters together in order to get a nourishing and hydrating lip balm that works for you.

16. Rosy Lip Balm

If you're a fan of rosy lip balms, then you've come to the right place! In this, we'll talk about a fun rose lip balm that you can try. The beauty of this one is of course, it's pretty simple, and it comes with some good ingredients that offer a beautiful rose texture to it, and of course, a sweet hint of vanilla, and the nourishment of cocoa butter as well.

This one is also pretty easy to use, and it offers a lot of great options if you're a fan of this type of lip balm and the fun that it has.

Ingredients:

- 1 tablespoon beeswax
- 3 tablespoons rose oil
- 1 tablespoon cocoa butter
- ½ tablespoon castor oil
- 1 teaspoon vanilla extract
- 1/4 teaspoon powdered alkanet root

Alkanet root will provide a nice rosy red color to the lip balm, and it's pretty easy to use.

Directions:

- Melt the beeswax and from there add the cocoa butter, the castor oil, and the rose oil to it
- For the fragrance, add the vanilla to it.
- Add the alkanet root powder for a natural color and from there, mix all of this together until it's blended.
- Once it's finally cooled down, put it in a lip balm container, and from there add it to the fridge in order to let it set.

This lip balm series is pretty simple to use, and they offer a lot of fun little additions. It also is great because the vanilla scent to it is quite pleasant and is good for you to use as well. Rose is also really good for skincare, and rose essential oil is one of the best for this. It does come with a blush color to it, so it certainly is quite fun and different. You can pair this in your favorite container, and it does apply clear to the lips too. Not only that, it provides excess nourishment for those who want something that is satisfying and hydrating to the lips and to help with chapped and dried out lips as well.

17. Hemp and Honey

Hemp is a natural ingredient that's wonderful for lip balms for the very reason of it's perfect for smooth, shiny lips, and also helps combat inflammation in that area too, so it's great if you have sore lips but aren't sure of how to heal it.

The ingredients are simple too, and pretty easy to get.

Ingredients:

- 1 teaspoon hemp oil
- 2 teaspoons honey
- 2 tablespoons cocoa butter
- 3 tablespoons shea butter
- 2 tablespoons beeswax
- 4 tablespoons almond oil
-

Directions:

- Melt all of the butter and beeswax together into the double boiler.
- Add in the oil and honey, and start to stir this until it becomes a liquid consistency.
- Add the honey to this, and then mix it together.
- For better blending, you blend this using a milk frother, and once it's medium thick, you pour the balm into the jars in order to set this.

This is a great one if you're a fan of hemp and hemp oil. It does have a bit of a hemp smell, but it's mostly masked by the other oils that are in this, along with the raw, natural honey that's there.

Hemp is known to be good for the body in general and is a natural skincare product. Many have learned that hemp offers some wonderful anti-inflammatory benefits that you can get ahold of and experience for yourself. That combined with the taste of honey makes it a skincare addition that you can enjoy, and one which is perfect for those looking for that one addiction that'll help their lips get the treatment and the health that they need.

18. Organic Shea Butter Lip Balm

Shea butter is really good for the lips, but did you know you could make a really organic lip balm out of shea butter? We'll give you another yummy shea butter piece for you to try.

Ingredients

- 1 tablespoons shea butter
- 1 tablespoon raw, organic coconut oil
- 5 drops lemon essential oil
- 1 tablespoon beeswax
- 1 teaspoon raw honey

Directions:

- Add the shea butter, beeswax, and the coconut oil to the pot and from there make a double boiler in order to heat the ingredients there.
- Once they're melted add the rest of the ingredients to the mixture to combine.
- Once cooled, transfer to the tubes and jars as you prefer.
- Use this whenever your lips are dry.

Shea butter is great for many things, including taking care of dry lips. You also can use this directly on cold sores too, and it will definitely help with putting forth a better, more rewarding experience for you, and for your lips as well.

Shea butter is wonderful for hydration and is one of the best ingredients for a lip balm. Not only that, it's also not too greasy when you mix it with this.

Lemon is great not just for the scent, but also for the health benefits. It's a natural antibacterial and antiviral, so it'll protect the skin from invaders, since the mouth is one of the main entrances to the body. But not only that, it also provides hydration and nutrients to the lips, offering a fun, immersive experience that'll help you really get the most out of this.

It is organic too, so you never have to worry about the chemicals in this affecting the body either.

19. Kool-Aid Lip Balm

Yes this is a thing. If you like Kool aid, or you have some of this lying about your house, then you should try to use this as much as you can. It's simple to use, and you can actually do it right now in your home. You can choose whatever flavor that you want to with this, and it's quite rewarding, and good for you.

Ingredients:

- A sachet of Kool aid of choice
- 1 teaspoon of water
- 1 teaspoon of regular sugar
- 1 tablespoon organic coconut oil

Directions:

- Empty the sachet into a bowl that's glass, and from there add sugar to it.
- Dissolve this by adding a teaspoon of water, more as needed.
- Add a tablespoon of the organic coconut oil to the mix and from there stir this until you've properly blended the ingredients.
- From there, let this cool, and then transfer to a lip balm jar and then store it until it settles down over time as well.

This is a great and fun one to try. It is a bit sweet, so keep that in mind. It is good as a general-use lip balm as well. This one is a lot sweeter than some of the others on the list, so you may want to be a bit cautious with how much sugar you use on this. but this is a good one for teens and tweens, and it does offer some benefits too, including hydration.

20. Limey Lip Balm

Limes are good, and you can get the taste of lime in your lip balm

This one only uses a few ingredients here, but they do work well, and are easy to mix. Lime essential oil has a lot of health benefits, and we'll tap into those health benefits as well throughout this.

With lime, you get a rich amount of antioxidants, and it can help with skincare as well. Plus, it tastes great and isn't as pungent as the lemon options that are out there, so it's a nice little change of pace for some people who usually go with the lemon option.

Ingredients:

- A tablespoon of coconut oil
- 1 teaspoon almond oil
- 5 drops of lime essential oil
- 1 teaspoon cocoa butter
- 1 teaspoon beeswax
-

Directions:

- To start, you add the cocoa butter, the coconut oil, the almond oil and the beeswax into a double boiler that's over medium heat.
- Stir this until it melts and then proceed to remove it from heat.
- Add in the lime oil and from there stir it together.
- Transfer this to the lip balm jars and tins, and from there, continue to let it cool before you put the lid on top of this.

You can use this for quite a long time, and it's a sweet, succulent sort of lip balm that's great if you're looking to add a lot more to this than what meets the eye. Lime essential oil is a little harder to find than some of the other oils that are out there, but it is available. If you really want to add a natural flavor to it, you can use lime juice.

21. Yummy Grapefruit Lip Balm

Grapefruit is another one of those great flavors of lip balm that people do love and enjoy. You can get this flavor through the power of grapefruit essential oil, and we'll give you a simple DIY recipe to help you get the most out of your lip balm. With this, you'll be able to harness the yummy flavors of grapefruit, and you won't be able to get enough of them! Plus, this is quite a simple recipe to follow, and a fun one to try.

Ingredients:

- 1 tablespoon castor oil
- 1 tablespoon shea butter
- ½ teaspoon grapefruit essential oil
- 2 tablespoons coconut oil
- Powdered beet root in order to add a bit of color

Directions:

- Take the ingredients and heat these up together. You should also incorporate a tablespoon of beeswax into this too for the added effect of the lip balm.
- From here, let it simmer until everything is melted, and mix this together.
- Once it's blended, you should remove this from heat, and from there add in the grapefruit essential oil. With this one, you only need to use a little bit in order to go a long way.
- If you're looking to add in some color, add in the powdered beet root at this time, mixing only a little bit until you get the correct shade that you're going for.
- Put this in some lip balm containers and then have at it!

50 Deliciously Simple DIY Lip Balm Recipes: Make Your Own Lip Balm From Natural Ingredients Today

This is a great one if you want something that's a little bit different, and it's a fun lip balm that you certainly won't be able to get enough of, and one that you'll get to enjoy as well!

Some also might like to put more grapefruit into there, and that's totally fine. It can get a little bit too sour if you're not careful though, so do exhibit caution when you do add grapefruit to this. but, if you're a fan of a balm being a little bit sourer and tangier, then you should definitely consider this yummy grapefruit lip balm.

22. Maple Syrup Lip Balm

You read that right! The yummy taste of maple syrup does work in a lip balm. This is definitely a nice, succulent and sweet flavor, and it's something that a lot of people really like. It is quite sweet, but it's kind of cool how you can have a sweet and syrupy taste to your lip balm right at your fingertips. How is it made though? Read on to find out!

To start, you'll need some ingredients. These are a little different from the other ingredients you might be used to, and you'll read them along with the directions below.

Ingredients:

- 1 teaspoon beeswax
- 1 teaspoon almond oil
- ½ teaspoon soy lecithin
- 1 tablespoon beeswax
- 1 tablespoon cocoa butter
- 1 tablespoon dark maple syrup
- 1 tablespoon cocoa butter

Directions:

- Put the ingredients together all in a double boiler. Let everything melt together, and mix it together constantly over medium heat.
- Once it's removed, whisk this together and continue to whisk this until this ends up completely cooling.

- When the mixture has cooled to room temp and emulsified, you can transfer this to the tins and jars and from there, have everything easily in one place.

This is a pretty simple recipe to use, but if you're someone who likes these kinds of yummy lip balms that are a little sweet but also quite fun and a good addition to this.

Make sure not to add too much maple syrup to this, since it can get a bit sticky and sometimes might cause the stickiness to transfer to your lips, which can get a little bit annoying. But maple syrup does offer some natural organic benefits, and the sweet taste and smell of it too is also a nice little added bonus. You certainly won't go wrong using this lip balm, since it does offer a lot of fun flavors, and is simple to use as well.

23. Orangey Vanilla Lip Balm

Do you like lip balms that taste like a creamsicle? Well, now you can get that through this great and really sweet lip balm. It's quite simple to use, and it definitely is a fun little addition to your lip balm options that are out there. To make this, you will need some ingredients, and they're pretty easy to get as well.

Ingredients:

- 1 tablespoon olive oil
- 2 tablespoons shea butter
- 14 teaspoon vanilla extract
- 1 tablespoon coconut oil
- 2 teaspoons grated beeswax
- 8 drops sweet orange essential oil

Directions:

- Put the beeswax, oils, and butter into the double boiler, and from there, let them start to melt over a medium heat.
- From there add the other ingredients together and then combine that together.
- Once it's finished, remove it from the heat and add more of the essential oil and the extract and from there stir this once again.
- From here, transfer this into the empty tins and jars, and then let it sit to use. You can work together in order to work on this, and that as well will offer a lot of great options for you, and you'll be quite happy with the results that come from this too.

Yes, if you're looking for a fun dessert lip balm, this is a great homemade option for you to try out as well. It isn't too sweet, and it does offer a yummy flavor and smell. You'll certainly enjoy this, and it's a good one to use especially if you have teens that want something a bit sweeter. But, all of us usually like some kind of sweet thing, so you'll be able to achieve that and so much more through these homemade lip balms, and you'll be able to do that with this fun orange lip balm with a strong hint of vanilla to it as well.

24. Lavender Mint Lippy

Do you like the taste of lavender? It's quite calming, and great to the taste. Not only that, it's easy to use to calm down, and quite simple to use as well. But you'll be able to get these sweet, succulent tastes directly from this in the form of a lip balm.

The mint that's added to add a bit of flavor to the lip balm, but it also isn't so overpowering that it's too much for the average person. In fact, it's quite simple, and very effective as well. You'll be amazed by the rush of both flavor and taste that comes to this, and the cooling sensation which comes from this too. You'll definitely love to use this lip balm, since it's so simple, and incredibly effective.

Ingredients:

- 1 tablespoon beeswax
- 1 tablespoon of coconut oil
- 6 drops lavender oil
- 6 drops peppermint oil
- 2 tablespoons shea butter

Directions:

- Take the beeswax, shea butter, and the coconut oil and then melt this in a tiny pot that' over medium low heat.
- Once you remove the container, work to add in the essential oils and from there, you should whisk this all together in order to distribute the mixture.
- From there, pour it into lip balm containers and from there, let it cool until it becomes solid.

You can use this every time your lips need a little bit of hydration, or if you're looking for a simple lip balm recipe, you have it right here. This one is pretty simple, but also incredibly effective, and is great for anyone looking to have a relishing lip balm right at their fingertips.

The mint might be a bit strong if you do end up adding too much to it, but in general it has that right amount of kick where it isn't much of an issue for most people. Do keep in mind that it might be too much if you go over the recipe, which sometimes causes a burning sensation on the lips if left overused, but for the most part, this is pretty good, and you can get the perfect balance of both.

Lavender is one of the best flavors since it is calming and offers a serenity that you don't get otherwise. It also offers a lot of benefits to your lips too and is naturally good for restoring health and beauty as well, which means it's perfect for those who want a good overall flavor that's calming and feels really good.

25. Easy Lip Balm

This is a simple lip balm, but quite effective if you're looking to add a DIY lip balm that's organic and really useful to the table.

Ingredients:

- 2 tablespoons shea butter
- 2 tablespoons pastilles of beeswax
- 2 tablespoons organic coconut oil
- 10 drops at least of peppermint essential oil

Directions:

- Put the shea butter, beeswax, and the coconut oil together into a double boiler over heat that's medium, and then stir this together until it all melts.
- From there, add at least 10 drops of peppermint oil. You want something a little less strong if you're someone who is sensitive to this. you should definitely test it on your skin before putting it in there too, so you don't use something too strong.
- Once the peppermint is in there, you should mix it together, and then transfer this to containers which are clean. Wait until this fully cools down before the cap is put on so it doesn't warp the cap.

26. Two Ingredient Lip Balm

In this, you'll be able to use two ingredients to create a lip balm. It only takes 20 minutes to finish, and it's great!

The beauty of two ingredients is you're not fighting with trying to find essential oils and the like, and because of that, it's all there. If you've ever been curious about trying homemade lip balms, this is one of the best ones, since this one is pretty simple to use, and you'll be able to, with this as well, create the best effects possible. You can always add more to this, and you'll be able to create a better and more immersive experience for your lip balms.

Ingredients:

- 3 tablespoons coconut oil
- 1 tablespoon organic beeswax

Directions:

- Use the double boiling system with a stainless steel or glass bowl on top. Melt the coconut oil along with the beeswax over low temperature and then stir these ingredients to combine.
- Remove from heat, and add any mix-ins as needed.
- Put it in tubes and tubs and set it aside for at least an hour or 20 minutes to set.

- Keep it at room temp for at least 30 days or refrigerated for 6 months.

You can add different mix ins including berries, sesame oil, cocoa butter and almond oil as desired. It also is good because a lot of people sometimes just want to see if they'll like this, and they may worry about an allergy as well.

If you have sensitive skin and don't want to sit there trying to battle with that, you can just add these two ingredients to it, and you'll notice the difference. While you're allowed to add more to this over time, sometimes trying it out to see if it'll create an effect is a good thing to do, and with two ingredients, you're not spending a ton of money in order to get a good result.

27. Cupcake Lip Balm

Cupcakes are great, and you can make an EOS lip balm quite easily with this. in this, we'll highlight how simple it is to make a cupcake lip balm, and just what you need to do in order to accomplish this.

Ingredients:

- An EOS container
- A small bowl or jug
- Sprinkles
- Coconut oil
- Vanilla
- A plastic knife
- Vaseline
- Beeswax
- Vitamin E capsule
- A bud of cotton

Directions:

- Use your old empty EOS container and or just take out the excess lip balm if you do not have an empty one.
- Apply a thin crease of Vaseline to the Eos lid and then sprinkles to where the crease is, and this will help put it in place.
- Take the rest of the ingredients and put them in a pot. Melt it using the double boiler method for best results.

- From there, re-insert the middle part and push the contents into the EOS container. Let it sit for a few minutes and then you can use it!

This one can be customized with different types of flavors too. If you'd like to add a more vanilla taste, you can always add more, but you can also add cocoa powder too in order to make it a chocolate cupcake flavor, which only adds to the fun of creating these great lip balms!

A lot enjoy the EOS lip balm cases because they are simple to carry, and they also aren't super huge. They fit conveniently in every container, and application is easier. Plus, it tends to hold the structure of the balm better whenever it gets warm out.

28. Crystal Light Lip Balm

It might seem strange to use crystal light with a lip balm, but this is great if you want something a little fruitier, and something that is indeed quite fun. The directions are simple to follow, and you'll get a lot of great benefits from this as well.

Ingredients:

- A package of crystal light
- Beeswax, 1 tablespoon

Directions:

- Take the beeswax and melt it over a double boiler method for best results.
- Mix in the crystal light, and put it together until thoroughly mixed.
- Remove from heat.
- Put it in the containers, and then place it into the fridge in order to cool. Usually after about 30 minutes, it'll be ready to use.

There you go! This is great if you have those lemony flavors or the raspberry flavors for the lip balms. Or, if you're just a fan of this type of drink mix, you'll be able to use this quite easily, and get a wealth of amazing benefits out of this as well.

29. Simply Lime Lip Balm

This is similar to the other lime recipe we have, but with a more tropical twist to the flavors. It's quite simple to do, and you can use these for personal use right away. It doesn't require a lot of time or effort when you're doing these, and that's one of the added benefits to this.

The ingredients are pretty standard, and you can buy all of them quite easily from the grocery store.

Ingredients:

- Two tablespoons coconut oil
- 2 tablespoons beeswax
- 10 drops lime essential oil
- 2 tablespoons cocoa butter
- 2 tablespoons almond oil

Directions:

- Take all of the ingredients but the essential oil and put it into a double boiler system. Stir all of this quite a bit until it's melted. Then remove it from heat.
- From there, add in the lime essential oil, stir it all the way in.
- Put it in some lip balm containers and then let them cool opened up for about an hour before you put the lid on these, since you don't want it to be sealed shut.
- You can use it whenever you want. These typically last about three months.

This is another fun lime flavor. It shouldn't be too much for you, but it does offer the fun health benefits of lime essential oil to it, along with a variety of other flavors to offer prime hydration to your lips as well.

30. Raspberry Lip Balm (with Real Raspberries)

You read that right. You can make a natural homemade lip balm that's made with raspberries directly. It might seem a bit strange, but it does offer a sweet, fruity taste, and it's quite different from those that only have a raspberry taste to them but aren't made with real raspberries. The color is also far more distinct than with the raspberry flavor, offering an even better, more rewarding experience for anyone looking to really get the wonderful taste of raspberries right there with them.

Ingredients

- 2 tablespoons coconut oil
- 1 tablespoon beeswax in order to create a firmer consistency
- ½ tablespoon freeze dried raspberries, adding more as needed

Directions:

- Take the raspberries and grind them in a coffee grinder until you have a really fine powder state with this.
- Melt the coconut oil and the beeswax if you're using a double boiler, and combine this together.
- Add in the freeze-dried raspberries and from there, stir it to combine.
- Transfer this to a container with a lid and then let it sit to harden and then use it as needed

This one does have a bit of a shorter lifespan of time compared to some of the other flavors that are out there, simply because you're using a natural ingredient rather than just an oil flavor. But these flavors are pretty great, and they offer a lot of good options for you especially if you're looking to really create a wonderful raspberry experience, and that of course is something that you'll definitely like to enjoy.

31. Plumping Lip Balm

One of the best ways to provide hydration to your lips is first to prep them of course, and then exfoliate them. Once you remove all of the dead skin, you can then let the moisturizers do the trick. You usually do this with a sugar scrub, but did you know that you'd have thicker, plumper lips if you use a natural homemade lip balm. You can plump your lips while also offering the healing benefits of this lip balm, and we'll show you how to make this right here.

Ingredients:

- 4 tablespoons coconut oil
- 2 vitamin E capsules
- 15 cinnamon essential oil drops
- 2 tablespoons beeswax pellets
- 1 tablespoon raw honey
- Lip balm containers
- Spoons to measure

If you want a firmer consistency, add more beeswax and reduce the coconut oil, and vice versa for a liquid lip balm.

Directions:

- Put the coconut oil and the beeswax together over a double boiler.
- Over the low heat, stir until both of these are melted fully.
- Remove this from the heat, and then add the vitamin E liquid along with the honey and essential oil. Put this in the containers.

- You must work quick, putting it in there and let it sit for 10 minutes before it hardens. Once finished, you can use this whenever you want to not only exfoliate the lips, but also to provide some extra hydration and moisture. Not to mention, it's made with the lovely fall scent of cinnamon too!

Jennifer N. Smith

32. Tangy Lemony Raspberry Balms

This type of lemon and raspberry lip balm has a wonderful pinkish hue to it, but also taste like lemons and raspberries. It's all natural and completely safe to use, and it's also quite quick to do.

Ingredients:

- Coconut oil
- Some lemon essential oil
- A bowl that is microwave safe
- Raspberry gelatin

Directions:

- Unlike the other recipes on the list, this one can be done in the microwave. First, you put this in a microwave-safe bowl, and mix it in there together.
- From there heat it for about 20 seconds, take it out, and then add the raspberry gelatin into this until it's fully incorporated together.
- Put it in the microwave once again and zap it for another 20 seconds. At this point, it should all melt away and become a deep color of raspberry.
- Take it out, mix it with the lemon essential oil.
- Transfer this to the lip balm containers. The color will be lighter than it looks initially since the coconut oil is transparent when melted and becomes a little bit different in color when it ends up being hardened.
- When pouring this, put it in the lip gloss containers. This one can be stored in the fridge or out in the open, and you'll be able to then take it out and use the small lip balm containers, or you can double the recipe if you desire to make more lip balms as needed.

33. Natural Hemp and Honey Lip Balm

This is a bit different from the other hemp lip balm, because this one uses specific honey and other flavors in order to make this really stand out. By the end of this, you'll be able to create the best and most immersive lip balm that's out there.

Ingredients:

- 2 tablespoons beeswax
- 2 tablespoons cocoa butter
- 1 tablespoon almond oil
- 1 tablespoon manuka honey
- 1 tablespoon carnauba wax
- 1 tablespoon shea butter
- 1 tablespoon hemp oil
- 8 drops of an essential oil

Directions:

- Melt the wax, butter, and the beeswax together in the double boiler along with the oil.
- Add the hemp and the honey and stir it in. honey isn't soluble with oil, so it won't fully dissolved and must be mixed with the milk frother.
- Remove from heat, then blend with the rest of the ingredients as this cool but then becomes pourable.

- Once it's thoroughly mixed, you can then put it into the tube sand leave it untouched to set.

The honey that you do use and the milk frother you add to it does change the consistency. It's better to use a little bit, since it does go a long way with the dissolving. This simple hemp lip balm also has the refreshing taste and benefits of honey. In general, you can also add the essential oils that you like to this, and it'll offer some great and refreshing benefits to this as well.

34. Wedding Favor Lip Balms

Yes, you can use this as a fun wedding favor. If you're not sure what kind of wedding favor to get someone why not tis? Everyone can use lip balm and it's so simple you won't regret even trying this, since it's very easy, and very worthwhile.

Ingredients:

- One lip balm base
- Flavor Oils of choice

Directions:

- Add the lip balm base to a double boiler base and use the chopstick to help with stirring.
- Once this is melted, add in the flavor oil of choice, starting with a few drops, and then adding more. You can add more for a heavily scented lip balm.
- Fill the containers with the liquid as the base to the height you desire.
- You can then print and create your own labels and put them on the containers, and there you go!

35. Sparkly Strawberry Lip Balm

Yes, you can add some glitter to your favorite lip balm. In fact, edible glitter is perfect if you're someone looking for that extra little shimmer in your lip balms. They are simple to make, and you'll definitely be amazed by how simple this is.

Ingredients:

- 1 tablespoon coconut oil
- 1 tablespoon beeswax
- 1 tablespoon strawberry gelatin mix
- ½ teaspoon edible glitter, more or less as needed

Directions:

- First, you need to take the oil and the beeswax and put it together in a container. Let it melt over a double boiler and stir till melted. Add in the gelatin, and then stir it until it's fully incorporated.
- From there, remove it, and add any extra essential oils to the mixture, and of course the edible glitter, stirring it all together.
- Once everything is mixed, you put it together into the containers, and then let it sit in the fridge, making it easier for you to use as well.

36. Simple Pink Lip Balm

Pink is a wonderful color! And of course, you can always get some great styles out of a fun pink tinted lip balm. Here is a simple DIY recipe for this.

Ingredients:

- 2 tablespoons grated beeswax
- 1 tablespoon coconut oil
- 2 teaspoons almond oil
- A chunk of some red lipstick, as much as you feel is needed
- ½ teaspoon shimmery eyeshadow in order to add some sparkle, or ½ teaspoon edible glitter

Directions:

- Boil the water in a sauce pan, and then put a metal pot on top to make the double boiler. Melt all of the ingredients until it's liquid, and make sure you don't overcook it since it will get runny and grainy. Stir it with a bamboo skewer for best results.
- Stir in the essential oil once you take it off the heat.
- Melt the liquid lipstick as needed in order to create the pinkish tint. Put the mixture into the lip gloss containers. Let it sit at room temperature or the fridge. If you need help putting it into those containers, just get one of those small medicine droppers to make it easy for you.

And there you have it! A simple pink lip balm mixture that's fun for everyone, and a good one to use especially if you're someone who likes fun lip balms such as this.

37. Coconut Rose Lip Balm

This is a sweet and beautiful lip balm that looks pretty, and actually tastes pretty too. The ingredients are available at most food and craft stores, and they are easy to put together.

Ingredients:

- 1.8 cup of coconut oil
- 1/8 cup shea butter
- ¼ cup rose petals
- 1 teaspoon sweet almond oil
- 1.4 cup beeswax
- 1 teaspoon coconut extract or vanilla extract

Directions:

- First thing you must do is measure out all of the ingredients and put it into a small container, such as a Pyrex container.
- Heat this on low and put this on top and mix it all together until everything is fully melted. Alternatively, if you don't want to use a double boiler you can heat this using a microwave in 30 second intervals until you fully melt the entire thing.
- You can strain the petals if you like, but they really add to the lip balm and make it pretty.
- Put it into a container of choice, and then let this sit and cool completely until it's completely ready to use.

This is a fun and simple lip balm, and you can use it to make a unique rose look to the item, which of course is something fun. For an added bonus, add some rose essential oil to make it smell even amazing if you really want to do that.

38. Cool Refreshing Lip Balm

For those cool days, a lip balm that not only hydrates the lips but also is nice and refreshing is a great way to go. Here is a fun recipe that you can try, allowing for you to have a smooth and refreshing lip balm that you can enjoy.

Ingredients:

- 8 drops of peppermint oil
- 1 tablespoon beeswax
- 2 tablespoons almond oil to help dilute the peppermint and make it more tingly than burning in terms of sensation

Directions

- Melt the beeswax and almond oil together in the double boiler.
- Then add the peppermint oil.
- Be careful when adding the peppermint oil in, since too much of this can cause a burning sensation in the lips.
- Put it into the containers, and then let it stand until it hardens up for best results.

This is a simple and refreshing wintery lip balm and is quite a fun little DIY lip balm that you'll get to enjoy and love.

39. Simple Three Ingredient Lip Balm

Sometimes you need to keep it simple, and that's what we're here for. While it is fun to put together many different lip balm flavors, sometimes the more simplistic solutions are the way to go. Here, we'll offer some fun recipes in order to try this, and you'll be able to use natural beeswax with this for an added effect.

Ingredients:

- A part of beeswax
- Some grapeseed and coconut oil
- Flavorings of choice

Directions:

- Grate your beeswax and then put that along with the oil into a container and heat it over the stove. Once this is boiled, let it sit there until everything is melted. You will need to make sure that you have an even amount of each of the different parts to make this lip balm as needed for best results.
- Add in flavors and from there, pour it in the container. Refrigerate for about 5-10 minutes.

So what can you add into this? Well, spiced coffee is a great option! Lemon is a good one too. Another cool one, is melting butter and mint together. You mix butter with mint essential oil, and it will help bring a minty and buttery sensation. Finally, consider cardamom flavor too, since this is quite great and does offer some wonderful health benefits too.

40. Bottle Cap Lip Balm

Bottle caps are simple, and if you're someone who still drinks bottled beverages, you'll have some of those right? Well, now you can have even more of them with this fun lip balm recipe. To make this, you'll want to use a simple flavor, and of course simple ingredients.

Ingredients:

- Oil, one part
- One part beeswax pellets
- Vanilla flavoring
- Mint essential oil
- Bottle caps of choice

Directions:

- From there, mix one part of the oil with one part of the beeswax, melting this together in a double boiler.
- Mix it together and stir it until all of the contents are melted.
- Now You want to add in the flavorings, whatever it is that you feel like you want to use, and place it all neatly into the containers that you have.
- From this point, slowly use a pipette or dropper to help transfer the contents from that over to the containers that you have.
- Let them sit either in the fridge for about thirty minutes or out in the open for about an hour or so. You can then take it out and use it.

This is a fun and unique lip balm idea, and not only does it taste good, it also smells good too, and does give a refreshing taste. Just be cautious with how much of each of the flavors you use, since it can be a little overwhelming for a few people.

41. Mint and Shea Butter Lip Balm

Does lemon and mint really mix? Well, it sure can! If you're looking for a unique and fun DIY recipe for your lip balms, this is the way to do it, and you'll learn here just what you can do with these fun lip balm flavors.

Ingredients:

- 1 tablespoon beeswax
- 1 tablespoon coconut oil
- 1 tablespoon shea butter
- 4 drops peppermint essential oil

Directions:

- Get the double boiler out and from there melt the shea butter, beeswax, and of course the coconut oil. You can create a double boiler easily with a mason jar and saucepan. From there, melt the ingredients. Once you have the wax fully melted and mixed, you can turn off the heat.
- Add in the rest of the ingredients and completely store them in order to incorporate this together.
- From there, put it into little tins. You can also speed up the process of hardening this by putting it in the freezer and fridge, if you're looking for something that's quick and effective as well.

And there you have it. The mint also offers a nice and refreshing taste to the lip balm that you're using, and that is definitely an added benefit.

42. Swirly Lip Balm

If you're looking for a fun looking lip balm, then you've come to the right place. This swirled lip balm is great, and there are a lot of fun little colors to try out. We'll show you how to make this one here, and some of the cool pizzazz that you can accomplish with this.

Ingredients:

- Lip balm base, a natural color
- A rose blush lip balm tint
- A yellow lip balm tint
- Natural sweetener or an essential oil
- Vanilla lip balm flavoring
- Small lip balm tins
- A melting pot or microwave

Directions:

- First measure out an ounce of the natural base for the lip balm.
- Melt the base in the microwave for about 30 seconds until this is fully melted, making sure you don't overheat. You can stir every 30 seconds, usually taking about 2 minutes to fully melt. Alternatively, you can melt this over a double boiler system.
- Add in the vanilla flavor. If you want a stronger flavor, you can always add more.
- You can then add the sweetener, adding maybe 10 drops at most. Too much can be too sweet, so adjust as needed. Stir this until it's

- always fully incorporated. You can put a little bit on the palm of your hand and lightly taste it, but don't overdo this.
- Take the lip balm and pour a little into a separate measuring cup and put it aside, and this will be contrasting in color for the swirly nature of the next step.
- From there put in two drops of the yellow lip balm, stirring to incorporate and then set aside.
- Add two drops of the rose blush color and then mix this to fully incorporate it and then set aside.
- Take the yellow color and pour it almost to the top, then let it sit for the minute, and then put little bits of red into the yellow containers using a pipette.
- You can then take a toothpick and then swirl some designs. Make sure that it's a little bit cooled when you do this, so it incorporates.
- Let it cool completely before you put the lid on. Then have fun using it!

This is a fun lip balm and a little different, and it's one certainly worth trying out.

43. Simple DIY Lip Balm

You can make this nice lip balm quickly, and we'll discuss how you can do this in a very simple, yet effective manner.

Ingredients:

- Coconut oil
- Powdered makeup for the color
- Beeswax
- Sweet almond oil
- Peppermint and vanilla extracts for flavoring

Directions:

- Add in the beeswax and the oil and mix it together until everything is fully liquidized.
- From here, you take your extracts and your powdered makeup and add it. The powdered makeup is of course used for color.
- When using coconut oil, always be careful not to add too much to this. the same goes for the extracts.
- You can separate the batches and use different combinations for both. The sky's the limit with this!
- Once finished pour it into containers and then let it sit until it's fully cooled, up to about two hours in some cases. Then have fun using your newly created lip balm!

44. Birthday Cake Lip Balm

Wouldn't you like to carry a birthday cake flavor around the form of a lip balm? Well, now you can with this handy little lip balm recipe that you won't be able to get enough of.

The ingredients are pretty easy to work with, and you'll be using mica powder to help enhance the coloring, which is of course pretty cool.

Ingredients:

- 1.4 ounce cocoa butter
- 1.4 ounce mango butter
- 2 beeswax pastilles
- A pinch of mica
- ¼ ounce shea butter
- 2 tablespoons fractionated coconut oil
- 5 ml buttercream cupcake flavor oil
- A pinch of purple pigment powder

Directions

- Weigh out the butters, and then combine them in a small container, then add the pastilles into there as well.
- Melt this either in a double boiler or a microwave in 30 second increments until everything is melted, stirring a lot.
- Measure out the buttercream flavor and put it into a pipette, then stir it directly into the lip balm mixture.

- Make sure to take a pinch pigment power and then add this to the lip balm directly. Add more or less depending on the kind of shimmer and color you want.
- Continue to stir until all of the ingredients are then incorporated.
- Use the pipette and then fill the containers with the balm, being careful not to fill them to the top.
- Let them sit and harden, and then you can decorate the containers as needed, such as with Washi tape. You can also use different forms of decorating if you feel like you want to take this to the next level and add some extra little additions to it too.

Birthday cake is a favorited flavor, and now you can take it in the form of a lip balm as needed, which of course adds even more to this than ever before.

45. Minty Chocolate Lip Balm with REAL chocolate

Do you love chocolate? Because I sure do! Well, now I can take that same sweet succulent scent with me in the form of a chocolate lip balm, and here, you'll learn how to make a mint chocolate lip balm in a simple, yet effective way. This one even uses real chocolate.

Ingredients:

- 2 teaspoons beeswax pellets
- 2 teaspoons chocolate chips
- 2 teaspoons of coconut oil
- 2 drops peppermint oil
- 2 teaspoons sweet almond oil

Directions:

- First take your beeswax pellets and put it in the glass bowl or a microwave dish. You can also alternatively use a double boiler too.
- Let it melt and then stir in the chocolate chips and blend it until smoothed out.
- From here, add in the rest and then melt it once again, combining it.
- Add in the oils, make sure they're properly mixed by stirring them to combine it all together.
- Put it all into small plastic tubes as needed or little containers.

If you want to add more to the recipe, you're welcome to. Usually a couple drops of peppermint is enough. If you add too much of that to the recipe it will cause a burning sensation to sometimes happen, and it's something a lot of people end up realizing over time.

A lot of people like this one because it is sweet but do keep in mind If it is too sweet for you, add more coconut oil to it to help offset that.

46. Two-Tone Lip Balm

Have you wanted to make two-colored lip balms? Well, now you can with this fun and handy DIY recipe that you'll enjoy.

Ingredients:

- A natural lip balm base
- A bubble gum lip balm flavoring oil
- Lip balm tints of choice (preferably colors which you feel would go together)
- Natural lip balm sweetener

Directions:

- Melt the lip balm base, 1 ounce. doing it in 30 second increments until it's thoroughly melted.
- Add in the flavoring to this. usually, you want anywhere from 6-18 drops for the best levels of flavoring, but again, it's up to you.
- Add in the lip balm sweetener after that. Usually, anywhere from 12-18 drops is pretty good for this, so stir it until it's incorporated. You can always taste test it too to see if it's too sweet or not but do be careful with that as well.
- From there, you want to take the lip balm base and pour it into a small container. Take a lip balm tube and put it in the middle, from there holding it there until it's fully removed. You might have to wait upwards of 2 hours.
- From there, repeat the other steps with the same amount of lip balm base you used before, but this time adding the lip balm tints

coloring blue, or the other color. You should've added the other color to the other lip balm base.
- From there fill the center of it with that other color, whether it's pink and blue, or blue and white. Fill in the middle, and then let it sit.
- You can use a heat gun or hair dryer in order to help smooth this out as needed.

This is another super fun type of recipe that's worth trying out, and a lot of people are quite happy with this one, simply because it offers a fun and really worthwhile DIY experience for a lot of people. It does take some time to perfect, but you'll be able to, once you're finished, create the best lip balm that you can using this.

47. Brownie Lip Balm

Wouldn't you love a Lip balm that actually tasted like brownies? Well, now you can get it with this wonderful brownie Lip balm. It's simple to use, and it comes with a simple recipe that allows you to get the most out of this, and offers a wonderful, unique flavor that you'll most certainly enjoy.

Ingredients:

- 1 tablespoon cocoa powder
- ½ teaspoon honey
- 1 teaspoon cinnamon
- 12 tablespoon melted chocolate chips
- 1 tablespoon beeswax
- 1 tablespoon coconut oil

Directions:

- Take the beeswax and the coconut oil and let this in the double boiler, mixing this together until It's thoroughly coated and put together.
- After you do that, lower the heat, and add the cocoa powder and the cinnamon together into this. slowly stir in more of the chocolate chips.
- Finally, add some honey good measure. Half a teaspoon is pretty good, but you may want to use more if you're a huge fan of honey.
- Once finished, you should put it into the lip balm containers and from there let it sit until it's fully hardened out.

This does create a very brown lip balm, and it does taste and smell like brownies. It also comes with honey, which is great for those if you're looking to have something that not only helps with moisturizing the skin, but also provides a lot of great benefits to this as well if you're looking at add more to your lipstick repertoire.

48. Coconut Honey Lip Balm

Do you like coconut flavoring? Do you also like honey? Well now you can add these two together in order to create a simple, yet very effective coconut oil lip balm that you will enjoy. The cool thing about this one is that the honey will go towards the bottom and separate over time, but the coconut oil does stay. More importantly though, it's a strong honey scent, so if you like this, then you'll definitely like it. The scent of coconut oil also goes well together with the honey, creating a good, refreshing favor that you will know and love.

Ingredients:

- 1 tablespoon coconut oil
- 1 tablespoon beeswax or beeswax pellets
- 1 tablespoon honey

Directions:

- Create a double boiler and heat up the coconut oil and the beeswax together. If you want more of a coconut flavor, you should of course, add more coconut oil to it as needed.
- Once it's thoroughly melted, take the natural honey and put it in there.
- After that, you should pour it into the tubes. If you feel like adding anything else, you are more than welcome to at this point.
- Let it sit for about an hour or so to let it harden, and from there you'll have a wonderful honey lip balm that everyone enjoys, and one that you certainly will love more than anything else. The taste of honey won't leave your lips, and you'll be able to relish in the benefits of the honey as well as you continue to use this.

49. Heart Lip Balms

Wouldn't you like a cute little lip balm in the shape of a heart? Well, now you can get that, and we'll go over how to make this here. It's actually quite simple and you can add your own flavors to these as well.

Ingredients:

- Rose blush lip balm tint
- Lip balm sweetener or essential oils to flavor
- Strawberry flavoring oil
- A natural lip balm base
- Small cookie cutter in the size of a heart shape

Directions:

- First you must make sure that you apply the right flavor into this. anywhere from 6-18 drops is ideal, with more of course adding to the flavor.
- Take the top off the lip balm tins and put the heart shape cookie cutter straight in the center. Put it to the side.
- Scoop out the lip balm base and slowly melt it and stir it in thirty second intervals until it's fully melted. You should make sure that it's properly measured out.
- Put the strawberry flavor oil in the melted balm bas through a pipette.
- In the same process, put in the sweetener. Usually, 12-18 drops for this is ideal. You can also test out how sweet this is by tasting this yourself, and then going from there.

- Once you're finished with that, slowly fill the base of the lip balm around the cookie cutter. From there, let it sit until it's fully hardened
- Very slowly remove the cookie cutter. It's best if you wait until this is fully hardened before you remove, so usually overnight is ideal for this.
- Once that's finished, you should fill in the center of these balms. Repeat the first few steps with the lip balm base, but after you've added the sweetening and the base, add the rose blush tint to this and from there stir it to incorporate.
- When it's at the desired color, use a small pipette in order to put it on the opening of the lip balm tin. Put it in the center, and then let it harden.

And there you have it! It's a great gift idea if you're someone looking to give someone a really nice custom-made gift. They are perfect for birthdays and baby showers, and the cool thing you can do is match the flavors but add different colors, or even use different cookie cutters in order to create a unique and fun design that you'll most certainly enjoy from this as well!

50. Blueberry Lip Balm

The best thing about lip balms is well, the creativity that goes into them of course! You can also use blueberries as well when you're looking to add some fun to your lip balms.

These do some with the scent of blueberries and the flavor of them too, and you can put them in any sort of container that you want.

Ingredients:

- 1 tablespoon beeswax
- 1 tablespoon jojoba oil
- 1 tablespoon coconut oil
- 2 tablespoons vitamin E oil
- Blueberry flavored oil

You can also add other essential oils if you feel like they are worthwhile here.

Directions:

- Take the oils and the vitamin E and the beeswax and put them in a microwave proof bowl. Blend this all together until thoroughly mixed pretty well.
- Put it in the microwave and then heat this up for 25 seconds and then mix this up once again.
- Continue to repeat this process until everything is mixed up and it's all melted.

- From this point forward, add in the blueberry flavor. You should be careful with how many drops you're adding since if you add too much. It can be a bit overpowering. Of course, some like a hint, while others like the taste.
- Once the blueberry is added, blend this all together until it's thoroughly incorporated.
- Take the small tins and put the blueberry mixture into the center of this. you'll notice a small purple tinge to this because of the oils.
- From there, let it sit in the fridge or out in the open until it's hardened up, and everything can be used

This one has a pretty strong scent and might be a bit more than you may be expecting. But, it's a great one, and it's one that a lot of people do enjoy, and one that a lot of people love since it does have a distinct blueberry scent and is quite yummy too!

Tips for Lip Balm Creation

So is there anything you can use in order to create the best lip balms out there? Well, we'll go over a few tips here and there in this section, along with a few things that you should learn and know about when it comes to creating the best lip balms for you to use.

First, before you use the containers for the lip balm, do make sure to take the time to clean them out, so if there was anything left in them, make sure it's properly cleaned. Another big thing is that they're dried. The water in that might contaminate the lip balm, and it does affect the overall integrity of the balm itself if you do have a wet container.

While you can store them in your medicine cabinet at room temperature, in order to keep the integrity completely, they're best left in the fridge. For same with actual preservatives and natural ingredients in them, it's ideal if you keep them in the freezer to keep them around for as long as possible.

With beeswax, sometimes you can use it in the pellets form. Sometimes you may use it in a block form. Regardless, it's best to either grate or crush the beeswax before you use it. Otherwise, it will take forever to melt. While the melting point isn't that high, if you have a big chunk of beeswax just sitting in there, it will definitely take a long time, and it's certainly not something that you may want to sit around and wait on.

The best way to solidify the balms is of course at room temperature. But, if you're pressed for time or you really don't want to wait, the fridge will definitely make them harden faster. But, never put the tops on them until they fully harden. That will cause them to warp in a sense, and you won't be able to close the balm.

You should try to not use the freezer unless the ingredients will spoil. That's because a lot of the potency is frozen out when you put it in the freezer. But if you know something is in there that'll go bad over time, you should definitely consider making sure that you do have it at least partially preserved as much as you can.

What's kind of cool about these homemade lip balms is that the coconut oil, cocoa butter, and the beeswax all have natural SPF components to it, so your lips will get sun protection from using them.

You can use little tins to put the lip balms in, but you can also use tubes and other small containers. You can even use little plastic containers and other small containers if you think it'll be good for you. Basically, the sky's the limit with this.

Finally, if you're looking to have less chapped lips, and lips that are properly moisturized, you should just start drinking water. While this can help, part of the reason why your lips are dry is because you're not drinking enough water. If nothing else, definitely consider this, since it is something that you may be able to get the full benefits out of, and something worth trying out.

The Best Lip Balm Ingredients

What are the best lip balm ingredients?

This is a good question. While there are a lot of options, you may want to look into those which are the best of the best, and those which will help you get the most out of you lip balm.

While it usually is the same for most of these, here we'll highlight some of the top ingredients that these lip balms should have.

Shea butter is one of the best ingredients to add to your homemade lip balms. That's because this soaks directly into the skin and creates a tiny barrier that'll seal in the moisture. It also comes with anti-aging properties, which is good for more than just your lips. It's also great for sensitive skin, so it is safe to use on your lips. It also has healing and anti-inflammatory properties, so if you know that your lips suffered from a trauma recently, this is definitely something to consider. It's considered one of the best additions to treatment for the body and is good for the skin not just on the body, but those on the lips too.

Almost all of these balms contain beeswax, and for a good reason. This is one of the key ingredients, and it's incredibly gentle on the skin. It helps protect the skin from harmful impacts of the environment, all while rejuvenating the skin and restoring life to it, and also offers healthy and fresh lips. It also is a humectant, which means that it attracts water, which is why it helps with hydration and is a key part of lip balms as well.

Vitamin E is another popular one. You can get this in the form of capsules that you can crack directly into the mixture itself, and it is great if you're looking to strengthen your lip balm. Vitamin E is a skin protector, and it protects the skin from harmful UV rays. It's also a good one for pretty much any lip balm, because it doesn't affect the taste or anything, but ultimately is good for you if you're looking to hydrate and rejuvenate your skin.

Green tea extract is another great one when it comes to adding healing properties to this. that's because it protects your skin from a lot. First of all, it'll protect the skin from UV rays and will hydrate the skin in the process as well. It also is great for diminishing signs of aging, and it comes with super powerful anti-aging properties. So, you'll look and feel young, and also provide numerous benefits and a wealth of health to your lips and body as well.

Another cool addition is of course essential oils. Essential oils include lavender and other types of oils which are great. They offer a wonderful flavor to your lip balm, and many different health benefits. For example, some of them offer a nourishing addition to the balm. Others will help with hydration and other aspects of this. some of them also are good for healing, so if you do have dry, damaged lips this is something which you can use to help with that. Essential oils are something that's simple to add.

However, if you do plan to use essential oils, please make sure that you have a carrier oil added to this. carrier oils are good because they help to properly dilute the solution, and it will help make sure that the effects of this aren't too potent. While they are safe to use, there is the problem that they can be almost too much for some people, so it's good to consider making sure that you have a proper carrier oil in place for you to use, and you'll be able to quite easily, without any problems at hand, create the best lip balm that you can with this.

Finally we have hemp. Hemp is from the plant with the name, and it's a big part of natural health and wellness. It's been used in everything from food to even in gummies and oils. It can help with inflammation and other issues, and also provides a lot of nourishment to the body. While you can get this in a variety of different products, you can add hemp oil directly to your lip balm to get the full array of benefits from this. it's best if you make sure that you use the oil, since hemp oil does have the hemp benefits in it, and it's also incredibly easy to mix. It also is the easiest to procure, since you can get it from a natural foods store, or even just from a CBD store in town. You'll be shocked at how much of a difference this does make, and if the smell is too much, a couple of drops directly into the mixture will indeed make it so much better and offer a variety of health benefits too.

All of these different ingredients are simple to use, but also incredibly effective. You can add these to practically any lip balm solution to add a lot of beauty and variety to them as well. You'll be amazed by the difference this makes in your life, and the fun that comes from this too. If you're someone looking to make homemade lip balms, you'll be able to do this quite easily, and you'll be happy with the results of this too. If you're curious, consider using different kinds of mixtures of these ingredients, or add them to practically any recipe that's in this book, and you'll see a difference.

Cautions with homemade lip balms

Lip balms are great, and they are simple to use, but also incredibly effective. However, there are a few cautions that you should take with homemade lip balms, especially when making them.

First and foremost, be careful with any container that you're using with this. a lot of times, they can be very hot to the touch, and you might end up burning yourself if not careful. With the double boiler system, taking it off can mean possibility for your hands to burn, so you should be very careful when removing this from a heat surface.

Next, when you add in the oils, do be careful. A lot of times they are quite hot, so definitely never touch an oil directly on there, since it can burn your hands.

Beeswax does take a long time to fully melt, so make sure not to touch it while it's melting. When you do mix it, do make sure that you don't mix too hard, for there might be risk of splatter. If needed, get a long spoon or a chopstick in order to mix it all together.

For best measurements and results, consider investing in pipettes. This is good for getting the best ratio of different types of essential oils and flavorings directly into the lip balm and makes them all taste great.

Before you put anything in the lip balm containers, make sure that you wash them down. Don't worry as much about anything else, but make sure they're properly cleaned. It isn't just from a hygiene standpoint, it's also kind of lip balm if you have something left in there, and it might get mixed with the current lip balm. If you're made certain lip balm flavors before and want to try something a bit different, you should always make sure that you properly clean these out.

If you're working with a mint oil especially, take caution with how much you're putting in there. A lot of people sometimes shy on the too much side of things, which means that a lot of times it can create a burning sensation in the mouth, and that can be a bit irritating.

While these are safe for consumption most of the time, try no to ingest these. Those that are made with natural ingredients won't hurt you, but it can be a bit gross.

Finally, if you're working with children, please make sure that you do supervise them when doing this. it can be a bit much for some kids to do alone too, and you should make sure they're properly supervised so that nobody gets hurt or burned.

Making these lip balms is quite fun, and they offer a variety of different ideas that you may not get to experience otherwise. But, if you're not careful it could affect you, so always make sure you take the right precautions.

Conclusion

Creating your own homemade lip balms is a lot of fun to do. For many people, this involves a lot of creativity, and you can take these basic recipes and try them out for yourself if you've ever been curious. You can work with these, and the cool thing is, you can adjust them as needed if you feel like you're able to create the best types of lip balm that you can, and some of the cool elements that are a part of this too.

Lip balms are great to help with giving your lips the moisturizing that they need. Plus, you can make different kinds that smell amazing as well. With this book, you'll be able to sit down, make your own, and have a beautiful result from it.

With that being said, the next step that you should take is quite simple. Start to make your own homemade lip balms whenever you want to. There are lots of great lip balms that you can try out, and lots of cool little recipes.

You'll have lip balms for every occasion, and they are also great if you're looking to create some great gifts for friends. Make them, and have fun making them, and you'll never be the same again once you start on the adventure of homemade lip balm making.

Jennifer N. Smith

50 Deliciously Simple DIY Lip Balm Recipes: Make Your Own Lip Balm From Natural Ingredients Today

Jennifer N. Smith

Made in the USA
Las Vegas, NV
26 December 2023